Zhang Zhihe

# UNVEILING
# GIANT PANDAS

China Travel & Tourism Press

# Contents

# Preface

My career in giant panda conservation requires proximity to this precious animal. My work has offered me over two decades to observe and get to know giant pandas. In these wondrous creatures of nature I have come to see those who have survived the flux of changes through approximately eight million years of evolution. They possess supple agility versus a perceived slothful appearance, sparkling wisdom against blackened eye patches, and a rich inner world against a simple black-and-white exterior. Thus, in me arose a desire to unveil some secrets of giant pandas and share their mysterious solitary life with a hope that more people will join us in caring about and conserving them and the already fragile homeland that we share.

Zhang Zhihe
June 21,2010

# Hermits in the Bamboo Forest

In the dramatic high mountains of Western China, in the secluded high altitude riverine valleys, and among the dense woods and verdant bamboo forests, are fascinating and mysterious creatures of the world, giant pandas, known in China as the "bamboo forest hermits". With an interesting lifestyle, pandas are solitary in the wild and seldom exposed to the outer world. The alpine forest is their natural habitat where they live and bear their young.

With their home in the mountains at the altitude of more than 2,500 meters, pandas live their lives in the remote forests of China. Here, bird songs echo in the valleys year round providing some of the sounds of nature. The fragrance of alpine azaleas pervades the forest, arousing the imagination of a beautiful future. When pandas are thirsty they have fresh mountain water. In their habitat gentle breezes flow through the bamboo forests, moistening, refreshing and keeping them cool. This is the haven of freedom in which they thrive if undisturbed.

Without dangers such as bamboo flowering and human encroachment of their habitat, pandas would not be threatened. Pandas would live a peaceful life, surrounded by plentiful food and safe serenity. They normally spend almost 14 hours a day looking for and enjoying their favored food. And, just as humans do, they spend between eight and nine hours sleeping. The rest of the time they climb trees, maintain their territory, and groom themselves to maintain their thick coats. Without disruptions, they live a relatively peaceful existence. Just as a Chinese saying goes, they are "as casual as a cloud and as free as a crane".

Giant pandas prefer to stay where the average yearly temperature ranges from 4-15 degrees Celsius. Considering their thick fur, one does not find it hard to understand their need for low temperatures. When the mercury rises in summer, pandas move to higher places for cooler temperatures. Sometimes they enter cold streams to cool off. Winter is an optimal season for them. They remain energetic and playful in the snow if the mercury does not drop below minus 10 degrees Celsius. Of course, in severely chilly weather when bamboo starts to freeze, they are wise enough to go down the mountains for warmth and food. Occasionally, they might visit houses at the foot of the mountains where they may take some food. Through eight million years of evolution, they have survived countless drastic changes and harsh climates – they have been able to adapt to natural environmental challenges.

Wild pandas have many neighbors. They include Sichuan golden monkeys with a snub-nosed face and soft golden fur, lesser pandas which are smaller in size with a brilliant red coat, and takins which look neither like cattle nor sheep. Sharing the same habitat, they each have their own niches. Giant pandas and takins dominate the ground and golden monkeys and lesser pandas take over the trees. In harmonious company, they take from the forests what they need respectively. However, not all inhabitants are as peaceful. Leopards, golden cats, and jackals are natural predators of panda cubs. Though not a problem for adult pandas, they pose a big threat to panda cubs which, without mothers' protection and instruction, are very vulnerable to these predators.

# The Mating
of the Giant Panda

Normally, female giant pandas become sexually mature at five years of age, while for males it is closer to seven. However, some individuals mature earlier.

From February to May, when the white snow covering the mountains begins to melt, glittering icicles on tree branches turn into beads, cuckoos begin to sing in the valley and azaleas blossom, and female giant pandas go into estrus.

At this time, adult and sub-adult pandas, males and females, who normally live far apart, begin the journey for a mate. It is not easy to navigate high mountains and dense forests in search of a mate. Nevertheless, they have their tools to attract their potential mates. Both female and male pandas leave their scent and scratch marks on trees or rocks, signaling their readiness to mate. Known only to other pandas, the signals serve as their unique individual signal as to their mating status. They also use vocalizations to attract pandas of the opposite sex. However, even when a potential mate is found, it is too early to tell whether successful mating will occur as pandas, female pandas especially, are particular about their mates. When a female panda attracts a host of interested male pandas, she will tree herself and observe as the males compete for her. In order to win access to her, her pursuers must challenge each other. Often quite a battle ensues. The generally docile males become aggressive. They fight each other, maneuvering their strength and sturdy bodies to compete for the female. Their barks and roars echo in the valleys. Sometimes, serious injuries result. The female panda sits aside, watching. Occasionally, the female's vocalizations cause, the male pandas to fight more aggressively until one of them wins.

At this time, some sub-adult male pandas watch the fight from a distance, along with young female pandas. Partly driven by curiosity, this precious opportunity allows them to learn some essential mating skills. When mating order is established, the female panda allows the winning male to mate with her. It is as if she knows that the strong winner must have the best genes and best potential to bring more vitality to her newborns and more hope to carry on her genes. In order to secure her chance of becoming a mother, a female panda mates with several male pandas during the breeding season. Only after the winner mates with her can other male pandas follow suit. And the poor final loser cannot but, watch the winners with her.

Generally, pandas are erroneously believed to be poor breeders. But studies show that this is a far cry from the truth. Field scientists once found that a wild panda pair attempted copulation 42 times within 70 minutes and succeeded 39 times. A pair in captivity was found to mate for 34 minutes.

# The Miracle of Life

After mating with the female in the spring, the male panda departs, leaving her the task of bearing and rearing the young. No sooner are they impregnated, than females have to eat more to store more nutrients for the new lives in their bellies. Throughout the rest of the spring, they eat many bamboo shoots. Tender, juicy, sweet and nutritious, the shoots are their preferred food. In June when it is summer, bamboo shoots are tall and not as tasty, they expertly select more nutritious bamboo leaves or tender parts of culm. In the fall, they first choose the bamboo shoots growing in of the season. Once a cub is born, a female panda has less time and energy to seek food, because the newborn needs her meticulous care. Eating more food in spring, summer and fall to keep enough nutrients ensures their survival through the winter, a hard time for them to find food in the snowy, high mountains.

In many mammals, the shape of the female's body will change during pregnancy. But pandas are different, even when they are about to give birth, their appearance and shape are almost the same as before pregnancy. They still appear round and fat! Pregnancy, giving birth and rearing young are difficult experiences, but panda mothers are incredibly responsible and caring. Soon-to-be mother pandas usually have no appetite for about 10 days before birth. During this period, they show no interest in food and reduce their activity considerably. Most of time, they lie silently.

Panda pregnancy is unusual. Generally, the gestation of humans and other mammals varies only a little, as depicted in the Chinese saying "Human 10-month-long pregnancy leads up to birth one day." But this is not true for pandas. Their gestation is variable and can range from 82 to 225 days, and once a rare 324 days. Strangely, the size and weight of newborn pandas are almost the same no matter how long gestation is. It is thought to be the result of a remarkable phenomenon referred to as delayed implantation of the embryo. Whether this is the case is being researched.

Mother pandas look fretful and restless several days before birth. In captivity they pace a lot and continuously bleat. Meanwhile, they collect dried bamboo leaves, withered grass and twigs, and place them in a dry and wind-resistant hollow tree or cave to create a safe home for the newborn.

After bouts of pain, a female panda gives birth to one or two tiny cubs. Newborns are vulnerable due to their incredibly small size. In captivity we have found that their birth weight ranges from 51 to 225 grams, with the average weight being around 120 grams, or about 1/1,000 of their mothers' average weight. This is the most extreme birth weight ratio among all mammals other than marsupials. It is hard to imagine how a tiny panda cub gradually grows to be a big adult.

The vulnerability of newborns is found not only in their body size. Some of their organs are not fully developed at birth. They are blind and their eyes look like two mildly protruding spots. They have no eyesight and their ears have no auricles. Their immune system is not fully developed. Their thymus organ (a specialized organ of the immune system) must continue to develop after birth. Panda mothers have to be vigilant to safely raise their newborns. It is a lot of work for mothers to insure their health and development.

Newborn cubs, however, are also tough. Immediately after birth, they struggle to crawl and vocalize loudly to keep the attention of their mothers. Their loud vocalizations sometimes startle first-time mothers. Infants will vocalize if they need repositioning, to eat, to be kept warm, etc, by their mothers. Mother pandas lick their newborn cubs with their warm and wet tongue, which cleans them, stimulates their blood circulation and makes them feel secure. Newborn panda cubs cannot pass waste by themselves. When mothers lick their ano-genital area, it stimulates them to release waste. Interestingly, mother pandas ingest their cubs' feces before they are three months old. This is why people rarely find the droppings of panda cubs raised by their mothers. This helps to keep them safe so that predators do not smell the droppings of a vulnerable cub.

Newborn cubs feel hungry about two hours after birth. For a newborn, mother's milk is the only source of nutrition and her colostrum is crucial to their survival. Between three and five days after birth, a mother's milk is light green, just like milk with some green vegetable juice. Scientists have found that the colostrum is rich in nutrients like protein, fat, vitamins and enzymes and antibodies which protect cubs from disease. The varieties and components of the nutrients are very complicated. Even today, scientists are still researching the composition of giant panda milk.

A mother panda has four nipples which are hard to see among her thick fur. While at birth a cub is tiny and cannot see or hear, they do have the instinct to find their mother's nipples. If they cannot find them, they will crawl within the limbs of their mother and cry loudly for help. Their mother will adjust her posture to feed them. A mother who has better maternal skills or is experienced in raising cubs will move her cub closer to her nipples. Once the cub touches a nipple, they stop crying immediately and nurse attentively.

Before they are able to hear and see, newborn cubs cry, smell and touch to communicate with their mothers or to adjust themselves to the changing environment. They utter different sounds to tell their mothers what they need when they feel hungry, cold, hot or when their mothers hold them too tightly. Gradually, mothers and cubs become familiar with each other and cooperate better after a number of such interactions and communications. Mothers become more experienced and are good at taking care of their cubs.

Newborns do not eat much. A 120-gram newborn cub suckles about 10 times during the first day after birth, taking a total of about 15 ml of milk all day. Their appetite grows with the passing of time. When they are three months old, they get between 100 to 300 ml of milk from their mother each time, with the average daily intake of 270 ml. At this stage, they drink milk just once or twice a day.

A newborn cub is pink, totally different from an adult. About 15 days after birth, black patterns begin to develop on the cub's eyes, limbs and ears and their fur gradually becomes thick. At about 30 days of age they start looking like the pandas we are familiar with. However, they cannot open their eyes until six or seven weeks after birth and do not develop their hearing until 60 days later. Usually, it takes three months before a cub can see and hear soundly.

A newborn's activity is limited. Generally speaking, the lighter the birth-weight of a cub, the poorer its ability to move around. Within the first 90 days after birth, a panda's movement is directed mainly by their mother. They are confined by their mother's limbs. As time goes by, their area of activity becomes larger. By the time they are around four months old, they can crawl freely. They gradually follow their mother to explore their surroundings. For example, they enjoy fresh air and warm sunshine outside their den with or without the mother's company. The mother stays near the cub. Whenever there is a sign of disturbance or trouble, she can run to rescue or give a warning to keep invaders away.

The time cubs spend with their mother is one of the most important periods in their life. It is the time to learn how to live independently. The mother is the teacher giving firsthand lessons. The mother teaches the cub how to elude danger, look for tasty bamboo and water and find shelter from harsh weather. Some scientists believe that some breeding behaviors may be learned during this time also. These are the survival skills cubs need for life. The cub grows and becomes stronger day by day, and becomes more used to their mountain habitat. When the cub is between 18 months and two years old, the mothers will force them to leave for an independent life because they are ready to meet life's challenges on their own.

# Unique Traits
# of the Giant Panda

# Wise Vegetarians

Pandas eat a vegetarian diet despite their short digestive tract, being only five to six meters long on average, and similar to that of carnivores such as tigers, leopards or wolves. Bamboo accounts for over 99% of their diet. Pandas in the wild eat more than 60 varieties of bamboo with about 27 species being favored. Bamboo, a fast growing plant, is widespread in mountains and valleys. Bamboo shoots, leaves, and culm constitute an endless supply of food. It may have been due to the turn from a carnivore diet to bamboo-eating that pandas have survived eight million years of evolution. Many so-called hearty animals of their era have perished because they failed to adapt to the changing environment. It is a typical example of the survival of the fittest.

Bamboo has a low nutritional content so pandas are quite selective about the bamboo they choose to

consume. They spend more than 10 hours a day feeding. To supplement their diet they occasionally enjoy a variety of wild plants like the Chinese gooseberry or wild parsnips (*Angelica sp*.). How pandas grow quickly from a weak, tiny cub to sturdy animals by feasting mainly on bamboo, the nutritional content of which is almost negligible compared with high calorie foods consumed by humans and other species, is an amazing feat of evolution.

Again, the amazing adaptability of this ancient creature is represented by how they select bamboo for food. They always know which bamboo is the most delicious and which part of the bamboo plant is the most nutritious in different seasons. However, in any season, anytime and anywhere, they prefer bamboo shoots most. Bamboo shoots abound in moisture, nutrients and sugar and must taste good to pandas.

A Chinese saying goes: "A workman must sharpen his tools to do his work well." Pandas have a unique pseudo-thumb, a rare case among mammals. This "sharpened tool" allows them to grip things as conveniently as humans and other primates. The way they eat bamboo is especially amazing in its dexterity and precision.

I n the wild, young pandas live with their mothers until they are between 18 months and two years old. In captivity, however, 90% of young pandas are weaned when they are 4-6 months of age.

Once young pandas in the wild leave their mothers, they live an independent life without mothers' milk, meticulous care or protection. From then on, they must exercise all they have learned from their mothers to survive.

For most of the year, pandas live alone in dense forests. They are extremely solitary, seeking food, playing, or resting in trees or rock cavities. Only in the breeding season in spring do they travel to seek mates. When adults are mating, sub-adults usually watch nearby to observe mating skills so that they can successfully reproduce someday in the future. For adults, mating only happens in spring. After the short meeting, the partners leave each other, each going their own way.

In ancient China, hermits were believed to be those who, armed with great wisdom, saw through the emptiness of the material world and retreated to mountain forests. They shunned public life to lead a life of serenity in either temples with the companionship of a lone light, or remote mountain forests where they ate only simple food and found a complete escape from civilization. In Chinese culture, giant pandas are often compared to hermits. They seem to understand the essence of life while braving changes over eight million years. They hide on high mountains where few people have ever ventured. They feed primarily on bamboo, seemingly diminished in desires just like that of a hermit. They are muscular and powerful but even-tempered, largely concerned only with their own affairs. They live in utter solitude in the company of flowing mountain springs and the shiny stars at night all the year round. Don't they resemble real hermits?

# Motion and Motionless Philosophers

In the eyes of many people, pandas appear slow and clumsy. Standing at a height of 1.7 meters and weighing on average 118 kg (males) or 97 kg (females), they seem to walk slowly and eat bamboo gently all the time. So, it is hard for people to imagine that they are actually agile and strong. Scientists believe that because they eat bamboo which is low in nutrient content, they slow down to save energy. Some non-experts say that pandas are foolish and lazy.

As a matter of fact, this is a misconception. Pandas are mostly sedentary but also move frequently. When they are at rest, they appear calm and peaceful. If they feel danger or if they feel happy, they can run faster than young humans. They are more capable than humans in their amazing ability to climb trees, cross rivers and clamber up mountain cliffs in dense forests. Pandas fine-tune their movement and rest to most efficiently maximize their limited nutritional resources. In the philosophy of Chinese kungfu, those who practice martial arts have to stand like a pine, sit like a bell, and walk like a breeze before they become kungfu masters. It is as if pandas have also endorsed this philosophy in their life.

Big and heavy as they are, pandas are perfect climbers. In the wild, high trees not only protect them against predators but also give them excellent resting places. In trees, they can breathe fresh air, enjoy warm sunshine, and have a commanding view of the mountains; keeping informed of what is happening around them. At times, young pandas stay in trees for several days, sitting or sleeping. When they encounter predators or chase each other for fun, they can climb up trees swiftly to escape their pursuers. They climb so fast that we must admit that we are inferior to them.

High trees in the dense forests are places for females to retreat when being pursued by males during breeding season. When males compete for mating rights under trees, females safely watch them fight, often from high in a tree. In 2007, researchers found that three male pandas chased and fought against each other in the rolling Qinling Mountains in Shaanxi Province in Northwest China. The winner mated with the female panda high up in a tree.

Pandas are clever animals with excellent balance. Sometimes they are seen swinging and tottering at the end of branches. Often observers think they are about to fall, but they know their physical limits through experience and rarely fall. They are well aware of the consequences of their actions and the limits to what they can do. When they sleep on trees, they often straddle the crook of two branches and embrace the trees in a comfortable posture.

# Philosophy of Black and White

No other animals have fascinated so many people as pandas. People, regardless of their gender, age, color, nationality, language or faith, become easily overwhelmed by their mystery and natural beauty.

The credit, it is said, is partially given to their colors. Their black and white markings, two prime colors of the universe, are vivid and natural, symmetric and harmonious, and mysteriously distributed. The pattern and composition, resembling the Chinese philosophy of *yin* and *yang* and coinciding with the Taiji diagram of Chinese Taoism, bring people a sense of natural ease, a pleasure both to the eye and mind.

The beautiful black and white pattern of giant pandas is extraordinary. The two colors, while in shining contrast, are in perfect balance. Pandas are adorned with innocent faces like children with adorable black eye circles, resembling the Chinese character for the number eight (八). Pandas have a pair of round black furry ears and broad shoulders. They look simple and harmonious as a whole, naturally formed and perfect in every way.

The layout of black and white markings corresponds closely to the philosophy of *Yin* and *Yang* in Chinese Taoism. They are in sharp contrast, while naturally connected, simple but profound. This is verified by the Taiji diagram of traditional Taoist

The giant pandas' survival strategy reflects Taoist philosophy. A Taorism doctrine goes: "The sage tries his best to benefit all and contend with none." Pandas eat bamboo and inhabit high mountainous areas, rarely struggling for food against humans or other animals. With large and strong bodies not unlike those of predators with sharp claws like tigers and other bears, they are however good-natured and non-offensive. They avoid the affairs of others and conform to the natural ways of things. This mirrors a way of life advocated by Zhuang Zi, a great philosopher in ancient China, who preached that human

hearts should travel between heaven and earth.

Evolving through a long history of eight million years, pandas have out survived saber tooth tigers and mammoths that once dominated the land, a natural symbol of the thought of inaction advocated by Lao-Tzu, father of Taoism.

Pandas are like non-verbal philosophers. They assert themselves perfectly by practicing minimal action. With their peacefulness, mystery and legends, they are made ambassadors of peace and friendship.

## Love for Water

In the wild, pandas live near streams so that they can drink water as they need. Even in the coldest days of the winter, they seek flowing water even if they must crack the ice on the river. They may take a long journey in winter from high mountains to lower valleys to get drinking water. Once they spot a water source, they may lie beside it to drink. Sometimes when they drink a lot, they stagger and lumber as if they are drunk. Scientists guess that pandas' fondness of water and their habit of drinking a huge amount of water may be associated with the fact that they eat much bamboo and need help with digestion and alimentation.

Their preference for water is also reflected in their fondness of bathing and swimming. In the summer, they often plunge themselves into water, sitting, frolicking or playing alone. Water not only helps them stay cool, but also cleans their fur and body. Even on cold or snowy days, they may enter icy water, despite the freezing weather.

It could be assumed that it is not easy for adult pandas to swim with such a large size and thick fur. However, the opposite is true, they can swim well. People have seen wild pandas swim across rapid torrents.

# Born to Play

Pandas, young pandas in particular, like to play. As soon as panda cubs are able to move, they begin to show their affinity for play.

Mothers are the first playmates for panda cubs prior to their independence. They chase after each other and slightly bite at each other. Sometimes young cubs pretend to be violent and charge at their mothers. They even tease their mothers and happily climb over their heads. Mothers frequently encourage their cubs to play, wrestling with them, caressing, licking, gently pulling them down from trees on purpose. Words fail to express such a mother-cub relationship. In the course of such play, cubs grow up and gradually become strong. They learn a lot about their environment from their mothers' teaching and examples, as well as the basics of how to climb trees, deal with danger and choose bamboo.

Loving and excelling in play, pandas typically love novelty and loathe the old. Captive pandas are often given toys, which is called behavioral enrichment. No matter how novel the toys are, pandas will be tired of them in just a few days. Keepers have to constantly give them new ones to keep them interested. If they do not have anything to do, they will become unhealthy psychologically, which would lead to abnormal behavior.

One of the cutest things that pandas do is somersault. When excited, they can somersault very fast, six or seven times in a row. Chubby and bushy, they look like a rolling ball.

Play is infectious for panda cubs. When they are together, several cubs often romp with each other. Seeing their funny and mischievous play, viewers cannot help but laugh. When alone, they do not bother to move as much, sleeping more. Young pandas in captivity seem better at understanding people. When their keepers stay with them, they get more excited. They often do not let go of their keepers, possibly hoping that their keepers, apart from just giving them food and drink, could play with them.

## Lifelong Learners

A s they are destined to live a solitary existence when they grow up, they have a lot to learn in the course of their early growth. Luckily, young pandas are fast learners.

Extremely curious and interested in everything, young pandas often learn actively of their own initiative. Cubs over four months old, who are able to locomote independently, will begin to inquire about their surroundings, exploring trees, flowers, grass, bamboo thickets and pools. They probe into everything they can find.

Take tree-climbing for example. At the beginning, they climb cautiously and slowly, particularly when they climb high branches. They are very smart and rarely take risks when they find branches too slender to sustain their weight. Of course, some unwary pandas suffer from their carelessness. However, they can quickly draw upon their experience and seldom make the same mistake again. As soon as they are familiar with the trees and their own skills, they climb trees expertly. In captivity, they frequently chase and frolic with each other in trees. Adults can even mate in trees.

Adult giant pandas are extremely solitary. Because they live alone, there are many life skills for them to learn, like how to eat bamboo, find water, avoid dangers, mate and raise their babies. Without continued learning, their chances of survival are very slim.

# Territorial Creatures

The territory for each wild panda varies from four to seven square kilometers. Generally, a male has a larger territory than a female. The size of an individual pandas' territory is quite small compared with that of other large mammals such as tigers and black bears. Despite the small size, they have their favorite areas where they can find thriving bamboo, flowing water and good hiding places. The territory of males often overlaps that of females. So when spring comes, it is easier for them to seek each other out. Females are found to stay in quite a small territory, mostly within a core area, often where a good nest area is located. Here, water, food, sunshine and the terrain are suitable for them to give birth. Natural rock cavities or hollow trees are necessary sites for them to deliver their cubs.

The territory of a wild panda varies from season to season. It depends on how difficult it is to look for food. In winter, it is not easy to find fresh, nutritious bamboo. They have to spend more time and travel a longer distance. Sometimes in the wild, encounters with outsiders are unavoidable as their territory sometimes overlaps. In general, they do not fight but keep away from each other. Pandas are reluctant to leave their home. Once they establish their territory, they rarely move elsewhere except in the case of natural catastrophes or human induced disturbances. Researchers once moved wild pandas to a new place, several dozen kilometers away from their original habitat. However, with dogged determination, they traveled a long distance back to their familiar home. It is interesting that they are so attached to their territory.

# Diseases of Giant Pandas

Do pandas get sick? Certainly. Despite their sturdy body, natural food and fresh air at a high altitude, they still develop various diseases like colds, pneumonia, diarrhea, indigestion, round worms, mites and even tumors or cancers.

Scientists find that captive panda diseases are mainly related to digestive tract problems while round worms are the biggest problem for wild pandas. In captivity, the greatest threat to pandas is infectious diseases triggered by bacteria and viruses, such as hemorrhagic enteritis caused by E. coli. Another fatal infectious disease for pandas is canine distemper, which threatens pandas as well as many captive or wild canine species. Unfortunately, there are no vaccines or effective treatment once pandas are infected. We can do nothing but take every possible measure to prevent pandas from deadly diseases.

# Questions yet to be Answered

Pandas have lived on the earth for eight million years. They are well documented in many ancient Chinese books. However, even now, they are a mystery and people are still learning about them.

The following are questions yet to be answered: How do they grow, stay healthy, and raise cubs with a diet of bamboo of which the nutrition content is low as their staple food? They have a digestive system of a carnivore like tigers or leopards, but they eat as herbivores do, feeding on bamboo and occasionally on wild grass, similar to what ruminants such as cattle and sheep do. Why? They appeared on the earth eight million years ago and have evolved and survived the changes in the environment. How have they managed to achieve it?

Even the classification of pandas has long been under debate among experts. DNA evidence leads most scientists to believe they are a member of the Ursidae (bear) family.

# The Future

As a flagship species for the protection of endangered animals, pandas are only found in China. They have been christened China's "kind animal" and "ambassador of peace" since ancient times. Referred to as the country's "national treasure" and "living fossil", they were integrated into Chinese civilization and culture several thousand years ago.

Today, pandas have first-class protection in China. A host of new panda reserves have been created to protect them and other rare animals as well as their living environment. By the end of 2010, there had been 86 panda reserves established, covering 2.3 million hectares, protecting over 75% of wild pandas. A recent survey estimates that conservation efforts raised the number of wild giant pandas from fewer than 1,000 in the 1990s to about 1,600 in 2004.

Since the 1980s, in addition to steadfast conservation of wild giant pandas, China has put many resources into research on artificial breeding and ex-situ conservation. By the year 2009, the number of captive pandas reached 294, and ex-situ conservation has become another promise for their future.

There is no denying, however, that challenges like the small population, human encroachment, fragmentation of their habitat, illnesses and predators still pose threats to pandas.

Fortunately, pandas have drawn unprecedented attention. Public awareness of wildlife conservation has been enhanced. With great effort, it is expected that pandas who have survived since time immemorial, will have a bright future.